Look, Find & Learn

World History

Illustrator: Jerry Tiritilli

Writer: Linda Williams Aber

Consultant: Darrell J. Kozlowski

Louis Weber, CEO
Publications International, Ltd.
7373 North Cicero Avenue
Lincolnwood, Illinois 60712

Permission is never granted for commercial purposes.

Manufactured in USA.

8 7 6 5 4 3 2 1

ISBN: 1-4127-1048-0

Publications International, Ltd.

CONTENTS

Finding Your Way Through World History

LOOK at amazing illustrations of key periods of world history… **FIND** all kinds of things hidden in each picture… and **LEARN** tons of cool facts about historic events—all in one awesome book! *Look, Find & Learn: World History* gives the lowdown on some of the most significant people, places, and dates in world history.

Each illustration is bursting with hidden items for you to discover. Some will be easy to spot, while others will require more effort—and maybe even a magnifying glass! Surrounding each colorful scene are smaller pictures with fascinating facts and amazing information about the time period, making each search a fun learning experience. The facts will make the

most sense if you start in the top left corner and continue reading counterclockwise.

In some cases we've altered history just a bit so we could pack in as much information as possible—and add even more fun for you! For example, in the illustration about England, you'll find Henry VIII, Elizabeth I, and many other kings and queens all in the same place!

Often you'll be asked to find more than one of the same thing. Keep in mind that even items that are only partly shown should be counted. If you're completely stumped, turn to pages 26–31 for the answers. When you've found everything and want more, turn to page 32 for more challenges!

So start looking, finding, and learning—the fun will never end!

You'll have tons of fun searching for the items in each scene. Remember to start in the top left corner and read counterclockwise.

The Mummy's Curse

There's nothing more fun than getting down in the dirt and digging for treasures. Ancient Egypt has hundreds of treasures—from the giant pyramids with the tombs of pharaohs, to a sphinx with the body of a lion and the head of a pharaoh, to the mummy with a curse that just wouldn't quit! Can you dig it? Tut Tut! Follow me and walk like an Egyptian!

Egypt is one of the oldest countries. Would you like to visit Egypt where you can still see the pyramids? Find the sand pyramid that two kids are making.

Ancient Egypt was divided into 31 dynasties, and each dynasty had rulers called pharaohs. Do you think the President is a god? Well, the Egyptians believed the pharaoh was a god. Can you find the pharaoh who is wearing a robe?

Egyptians believed in life after death. They preserved the bodies of the Royal Family by mummification and buried them in pyramids. Even daddies were mummies. Where are the two mummies wrapped in white cloth?

The 4th dynasty pharaoh was named Khufu, but later he was renamed Cheops. He wanted to build the largest pyramid of all. Cheops ordered thousands of workers to cut blocks of limestone from a nearby quarry. Locate the worker who is sleeping next to a block of rock.

When archaeologists opened Cheops' tomb thousands of years later, there was no trace of the pharaoh. Many people thought he came back to life. The ankh is the Egyptian emblem of life. Locate the ankh symbol in two places.

 When King Tut's tomb, his mummy, and 3,000 treasures were discovered in 1922, they were considered the most important find of the century. Try to find his throne.

 Do you know that the most famous pharaoh of all was a boy about your age? Tutankhamun was only nine years old when he became king. He is called King Tut. Where is Tut's royal headpiece?

The sphinx is another Egyptian marvel. Unlike the Greek sphinx, which was female, the Egyptian sphinx was a creature with the body of a lion and the head of a man, ram, or hawk. Find the three Egyptian sphinxes. One may be easy to find, but look carefully for the other two.

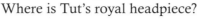

OASIS CAFE

In A.D. 1799, one of Napoleon's soldiers discovered a black stone called the Rosetta Stone. A French scholar, Jean Champollion, figured out what the pictures on the stone meant and unlocked the mystery of Egypt's history. Spot the fascinating Rosetta Stone.

Do you like to send messages to your friend with pictures? In the Egyptian tombs, the walls were covered with pictures, called hieroglyphs, which stood for a word or an idea. Look for a tablet with hieroglyphs on it.

 Scarabs were special stones symbolizing rebirth. The ancient Egyptians also wore the scarabs as ornaments. Search for four beetle-shaped scarabs.

 Some Egyptian queens, like Cleopatra, are just as famous as the pharaohs. Cleopatra supposedly killed herself by letting a poisonous snake bite her. Find the four snakes, called asps, before they find you.

The Sleeping Dragon

Like a sleeping dragon, the Great Wall of China snakes its way across northern China for thousands of miles. It is as mysterious today as it was more than 2,000 years ago. Let's go to China and find out why it was built. At the same time, we'll discover other marvelous facts about the ancient Chinese.

The Chinese built walls along their borders as early as the 600s B.C. to protect their farms from invaders like the Mongols and the Huns. Look for three Mongolian invaders.

In 246 B.C., the 14-year-old son of a prince in the province of Qin named himself Qin Shih Huang Ti—First Sovereign Emperor. Qin, pronounced *Chin*, was the source for the name "China." Where is Emperor Qin?

Qin was the ruler of rulers. He devised Chinese writing, money, and measurements. He also formed an army that took away the land of 120,000 nobles who lived nearby. He melted their weapons and had them made into bells. Can you find three bells?

Qin was a cruel ruler who readily killed or banished those who opposed him. Just to be safe, he burned records that remained from previous regimes so that his people and future generations would remember only him and none of the earlier rulers. Look for three burning records.

The Chinese word for palace is "gong." Qin built a "gong" that was two miles long and 1,000 paces wide. Where's the other kind of gong—the noisy kind?

The Ancient Chinese believed the number "9" was the symbol for the supreme sovereignty of the emperor. Towers were built to show military strength. Find nine towers.

Eventually the Great Wall of China was extended to 4,000 miles long. That's longer than driving straight across the United States. Find the person wearing a shirt with a painting of a wall on it.

The wall was supposed to have a watchtower about every one hundred yards, and the watchtowers were to be 40 feet high so soldiers could watch for approaching enemies. Eventually there were 25,000 towers. Find a soldier blowing a bugle to alert the people to oncoming danger.

Emperor Qin had a fantastic idea. He would connect all the old walls across the country and add new sections to make a Great Wall of China. To mark the route, he fastened a saddle to his horse and wherever the horse dragged it would mark the route of the Great Wall. Can you find this horse?

The workers built wood or bamboo frames, packed the frames with earth, and pounded them into various places in the Wall. Peasants also pushed small handcarts with stones to masons, who placed the stones on top of each other. Find the cart with three rocks.

Qin had many wives but only one empress. They all lived in the palace. To keep the marble floors clean, they were required to leave their shoes at the door. Do you take off your shoes in your house? Can you find a pair of ladies' red slippers with yellow designs?

The emperor's guardian god was the dragon. Gold dragons decorated the outside walls of the palace and wrapped around the columns inside. Qin sat on a dragon throne and wore a dragon robe. Don't be draggin' your heels when it comes to finding the red dragon.

Ten Famous Greeks

During the Golden Age of ancient Greece, ten Greeks came up with ideas we live by today. Did you know we got the word "democracy" from the Greek word *demokratia,* which means "power to the people"? Take a look at Athens in ancient times, and see how the Greeks touch our lives in other ways.

 What is the most important site in your city or town? In ancient Athens, it was the Acropolis, which was called the "Sacred Rock" of Athens. Rock 'n' roll, and find four large rocks in this scene of the Acropolis.

The Parthenon stands on the Acropolis and was built between 447 and 438 B.C. It is the most famous monument of the ancient Greek civilization. It will be a monumental success if you find a miniature Parthenon.

The Greeks named their most famous city after Athena, the Greek goddess of wisdom. According to myth, she struck the ground with a lightning bolt, and an olive tree sprouted up. Olive trees provide oil for cooking, olives to eat, and wood to build homes. A boy is climbing one of those olive trees. Can you find him?

 One of the world's greatest poets was Homer, who probably lived in the ninth or eighth century B.C. He wrote *The Iliad* and *The Odyssey*. Look for Homer, who might appear as though he is horsing around.

Aeschylus (525–456 B.C.) was the first playwright to give dignity and meaning to tragedy. But his death was a little less dignified. An eagle mistook his bald head for a stone and dropped a tortoise on it to break its shell. Use your eagle eye to find his bald head.

 Two other important Greeks were Pythagorus (580–500 B.C.), who developed the principles of geometry, and Hippocrates (460–377 B.C.), who advanced the study of medicine. Study this scene to find Pythagorus.

 Aristotle (384–322 B.C.), a student of Plato, studied governments of the past. And unlike others of his time, he believed the earth was round. Turn around and find an ancient globe that isn't round.

 Although Socrates never wrote anything down, his student Plato (428–348 or 347 B.C.) did. Plato is best known for his book *The Republic*, a record of Socrates' conversations with other Athenians. In Plato's ideal society, men and women are treated equally. Get to work finding a man and a woman doing the same job in this scene.

 Socrates (470–399 B.C.) was the first great Greek philosopher. He was very smart and often dressed like a beggar. He also poked fun at people in power, which led to his arrest. After being forced to drink hemlock, which is a poison, he died. Cheers to you if you find Socrates holding a cup.

 For 40 years, Aristophanes (450–388 B.C.) was a great comedy writer. He loved to poke fun at society and well-known politicians. Laugh if you will, but find the laughing Aristophanes.

 Sophocles (496–406 B.C.) is also famous for his tragedies. A tragedy is a play about the downfall of a great person. Sophocles had another talent; he was a fine dancer. It would be tragic not to find him in this scene.

 Euripedes (484–406 B.C.) wrote great tragic plays and was known for being the saddest of all the Greek playwrights. He was able to make people feel compassion for the suffering of others. Dry your eyes, and find three crying people.

VESUVIUS ERUPTS

When in Rome, do as the Romans do. Go to the chariot races. Cheer for your favorite gladiator at the Colosseum. Or if you're one of the wealthier Romans, spend your summer vacation in the resort towns of Pompeii or Herculaneum. But pay attention to the earth's rumblings. You could be in deep trouble!

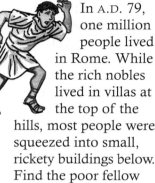

In A.D. 79, one million people lived in Rome. While the rich nobles lived in villas at the top of the hills, most people were squeezed into small, rickety buildings below. Find the poor fellow who has to duck under a low doorway.

From the Imperial Box at the Circus Maximus, the emperor and empress would watch the chariot races. They had the best view in the arena. Stop lyin' around, and find the chariot that pictures a lion.

In the violent show at Rome's Colosseum, gladiators often fought each other to the death. At other times, savage animals pounced upon captured enemies of the Roman Empire to the delight of the roaring crowd. Find the animal attacking the prisoner in the Colosseum.

In the summer, nobles left Rome's heat and traveled 100 miles south to villas in resort towns such as Pompeii and Herculaneum. But even in Pompeii, they could watch gladiators fight in the city's amphitheatre. Can you find three gladiators' shields on the ground together?

Rumblings from Mount Vesuvius were common for the people who lived in Pompeii and Herculaneum. On the morning of August 24, 79 (A.D.), many of the residents were not alarmed when their homes shook. Don't just sit there—find the chair that fell over.

A museum in Pompeii holds death casts of some of those who perished. Volcanic ash formed plaster molds of their bodies. One cast is of a watchdog still chained to a post at the entrance of a house. Can you sniff out three dogs in this scene?

A fisherman named Pliny the Younger wrote an eyewitness account of the volcano: "A tall cloud, shaped like a pine tree, rose from the top of Mount Vesuvius. Parts of the cloud were very bright, and parts were quite dark." Can you find Pliny the Younger?

In some parts of Pompeii, the volcanic ash and cinders were lighter than at Herculaneum, and after the eruption, some homeowners were able to dig out a few treasured possessions. Can you dig up four shovels?

Over most of Herculaneum, the ash, lava, and steam from Mount Vesuvius combined to form a layer of rock that was 65 feet deep, which made excavation impossible. Have you ever tried to crack solid rock with a pick? Take a crack at picking out a broken pick in this scene.

For three days it was as black as midnight. Molten lava flowed from Vesuvius and covered Pompeii and Herculaneum. Its force was so great that it crushed many buildings. Yet in other places it was so light that it left plates unbroken. Find an unbroken plate.

Vesuvius gave Pompeiians clues that an eruption was coming. Small quakes shook the area. Wells dried up, and springs stopped flowing. Dogs howled, and birds were silent. You'd do well to find three wells.

As night fell, huge flames shot out of Vesuvius. Sixty gladiators perished in their barracks, and some of the wild animals broke loose. Can you catch a tiger that has escaped?

Sail the high Seas

Between A.D. 800 and 1100, fierce Vikings from Norway, Sweden, and Denmark sailed the seas in search of land, wealth, and power. They swept across Europe and North Africa, attacking villages, taking what they wanted, and destroying the rest.

Vikings were very superstitious and believed in luck. They also worshiped many gods. One of their favorites was Mighty Thor, the god of war. Don't get knocked on the head when you look for him.

The Vikings were skilled mariners. They sailed across the high seas in wooden boats called longships. These boats were about 75 feet long and made out of oak. The Vikings shaped them like serpents or dragons. It won't take you long to find the longship with this sail.

People once thought the world was flat. They believed if you sailed too far, you would fall off the edge of the earth into a dark hole filled with dragons and sea serpents. The one-eyed god Odin, the supreme god of Norse mythology, is trying to send a ship over the edge. Where is he blowing?

The Vikings developed navigational techniques that were very advanced. For example, they used a sunstone to locate the sun when the sky was overcast. It worked like the twilight compass that guides jets across the polar ice cap today. Use your compass and find three sunstones.

The Danes settled in Normandy, France, bringing Viking customs to the Normans. William the Conqueror rose to power in Normandy but continued Viking traditions. Search for this famous conqueror.

The Vikings loved heroic stories, or *sagas*. One saga tells of Olaf the Stout, who sailed his ship under London Bridge. His men tied ropes to the posts and rowed downstream, pulling down the bridge. This tale inspired the nursery rhyme "London Bridge Is Falling Down." Cross this stone bridge when you come to it.

The Vikings had a passion for poetry. Every king had his personal *skald* (poet), who wrote about his deeds of derring-do. No king would go into battle without his skald. Locate three skalds (hint: they are wearing brown caps and brown garments).

Women cooked the meals, washed the clothes, cleaned the house, and milked the goats. In her spare time, a wife combed her husband's hair. Vikings were very proud of their long blond locks. Comb through this picture to find five combs.

The Norse built timbered houses and barns, tended oxen, and plowed fields. They worshiped Frey, the god of fertility, and asked that he bless their crops and live-stock. Don't be afraid to find Frey.

The Vikings developed their own alphabet, which looked like twigs and scratch marks. The letters were called *runes* and were thought to have magic meaning. The Vikings left runes on stones and carved messages in trees. Run, don't walk, to find a rune.

The Vikings were always hunting for gold. When they weren't raiding cities along the coast of France, Portugal, or Spain, they were trading furs from Scandinavia for golden jewelry and cups. Look for three golden goblets.

When France wouldn't let the Vikings sail up the River Seine in A.D. 855, the Danes came with 200 ships and attacked the Ile de la Cité, an island in the center of Paris, burning churches and killing priests. They also destroyed books and relics. Try to come across a silver cross.

AN ISLAND NATION

If you saw a golden eagle with a rattlesnake in its mouth, sitting on a cactus in a marshy area infested with mosquitoes, would you think that was a good place to build your house? The Aztecs did! They thought it was a sign from the god Huitzilopochtli (pronounced weet-see-loh-PAWCH-tlee, which means hummingbird-on-the-left). You won't believe what other things they believed!

The Aztecs moved from place to place until they settled in Mexico. They built a city on an island in Lake Texcoco in 1325 and named their city Tenochtitlán. According to legend, the gods told them to build their city at the spot where an eagle is eating a snake on a cactus. Can you find a picture of this legendary scene?

At one time, more than 300,000 Aztecs lived in Tenochtitlán, which had pyramids and palaces many centuries ago. Some think that growing vegetables in water is a modern idea, but the Aztecs grew floating gardens. Where are two baskets full of vegetables?

When they ran out of space on the island, the Aztecs used their canoes to collect sticky mud from the lake. They then dumped the mud onto large rafts made of reeds and weeds, so they could grow plants. Can you find four canoes?

Vegetables, flowers, and even trees were grown on these floating rafts, called *chinampas*. The plant roots would grow through the mats and down into the water. The roots joined the chinampas together to form floating islands. Can you find this flowering bush on a chinampa?

In 1503, Montezuma II was emperor of the Aztecs. His palace was in Tenochtitlán. The palace contained the imperial suites, the high courts, the war council, the treasury, and the prison. Where is Montezuma's crown of gold and green feathers?

Cortés took Montezuma II prisoner in his own palace and took his treasures. After many battles, the Spaniards destroyed the Aztec Empire in 1521. The leaders of the Spanish conquerors were known as *conquistadors*. Spanish priest Bartolome Casas objected to the conquistadors' treatment of the Aztecs and tried to be kind to them. Kindly find him.

Montezuma II treated Cortés with great courtesy, even showing him all the gold in his palace. Can you find the gold incense burner that dazzled Cortés?

On November 8, 1519, the Spanish explorer Hernán Cortés and his soldiers came to Tenochtitlán. Seeing Cortés on his horse and in his armor, Montezuma II thought Cortés was the god Quetzalcoatl returning to reclaim his kingdom. Do you see his white horse?

At an Aztec academy, the boys learned military duties. They also learned proper behavior, reading and writing, priestly rituals, and agriculture. At night, they danced and sang while others banged on drums and blew into conch shells to make music. Where is the boy blowing into a conch shell?

The instruction of Aztec children was strict. If they misbehaved, they were scratched with cactus thorns. Girls helped their mothers with housework and were taught to weave. Boys carried water and wood and learned to fish. Find the girl sewing a cloth.

Huitzilopochtli was the god of war and the noonday sun, and his temple was built next to the palace. Priests of the temple had to know the stars and the planets. Gaze at the priest with stars on his clothing.

The Aztecs believed Quetzalcoatl, the Feathered Serpent, was the god of the wind, the sun, and the planet Venus. According to Aztec legend, Quetzalcoatl had been a man of generosity and beauty but was forced to leave his kingdom. Look for the serpent with green feathers.

Life in the Middle Ages

In the Middle Ages (500–1500 A.D.), most of the land in Europe belonged to kings. A king gave some of his land, called a "fief" (pronounced FEEF), to strong and powerful noblemen called "lords." In exchange, they pledged to defend the king against his enemies. On his fief, each lord built a castle for his family, where his knights, merchants, and servants also lived.

Building a castle could take more than 20 years. Once completed, guards took turns looking out for the enemy on the battlements of the castle walls. If a castle was attacked, archers would defend it. Target the archer defending this castle.

To enter the castle yard, visitors had to cross a drawbridge over a "moat." A moat is a very deep, wide ditch filled with water. In case of attack, the drawbridge could be pulled up so that no one could get in—not even a duck or swan. Duck if the drawbridge drops as you look for three black swans.

In the towers, the lord and lady of the castle had private apartments joined by spiral staircases, which usually turned to the right. This way, an attacker climbing the stairs would not have room to swing his sword if he was right-handed. Take a swing at finding this attacker who snuck into the castle.

In the Middle Ages, people ate breakfast at sunrise, dinner at midday, and supper around sundown. Instead of plates, they ate on thick slices of stale bread called "trenchers." Soggy trenchers were given to beggars. Find a beggar with a trencher.

The Christian faith was very important to medieval Europeans. In fact, the lord and lady of the castle often went to the castle's chapel for morning worship. Each castle had its own priest in whose care was the Holy Bible. Care to locate three Bibles?

After dinner, the lord sometimes led his guests on a hunt through the forests. He used trained falcons and hawks to catch smaller birds and rabbits. The "mews" is where the falcons were kept. Amuse yourself—find the falcon in its mews.

To entertain the king and his guests, traveling actors performed religious plays, and traveling musicians sang songs and told stories of famous battles. The court often had "court jesters" as well. Entertain yourself by finding two jesters in this scene.

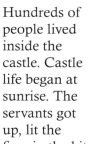

Hundreds of people lived inside the castle. Castle life began at sunrise. The servants got up, lit the fires in the kitchen and Great Hall, and got the morning meal under way. Floors had to be swept and basins washed. Shed some light on the chandler making candles for the chandeliers in the Great Hall.

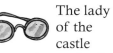

The lady of the castle oversaw the work of the chambermaids and the kitchen staff. She supervised her large group of spinners, weavers, and embroiderers, who made clothing for everyone in the castle. Luckily, eyeglasses were invented in the Middle Ages so people with poor eyesight could sew! Try not to squint to see a set of eyeglasses.

A squire could be dubbed a knight at 21. During peacetime, knights competed in mock battles, called tournaments, to display their bravery and honor, and to practice for war. "Jousts" were two-man contests in which two knights on horseback raced head-on trying to unseat one another with wooden lances. You have a fighting chance to find the lance not being used in the joust.

At 14, some boys became squires. A squire, under the guidance of a knight, studied manners, swordplay, and horsemanship. The squire cared for the knight's horses and polished his weapons and armor. You won't have to run the gauntlet to find the knight's metal gloves called "gauntlets."

The lord of the castle performed many duties. In this scene, he is knighting one of his squires. It was an honor to serve the lord as a squire but an even greater honor to be a knight. Would you do the honors of finding the lord of this castle?

THE RENAISSANCE | A Celebration of Life

During the fourteenth, fifteenth, and sixteenth centuries, many people throughout northern and western Europe changed the way they thought about life. Rather than worry about getting to heaven, they celebrated life on earth. Artists and sculptors reflected this new thinking through magnificent works of art. Take a stroll through this museum to learn more!

"Renaissance" comes from the French word meaning "rebirth." After a perceived decline in the arts during the Middle Ages, Renaissance scholars, sculptors, and painters sought to revive the great works of ancient Greece and Rome. Search for the statue of the Greek god Apollo.

Although artists still worked for the Church as in the Middle Ages, they didn't depend on the Church to make their livings. Wealthy patrons like the Duke of Urbino of the Medici family supported them. Draw upon your powers of observation to find Piero della Francesca's (1416–1492) portrait of the duke.

Jan van Eyck (c. 1390–1441), a Dutch painter, created a new kind of paint that mixed colored powders with oil. Artists could blend the colors to create a three-dimensional look. A dog like the one in van Eyck's painting, *Arnolfini Wedding,* is running in this museum. You'll be top dog if you find it!

Filippo Brunelleschi (1377–1466) discovered that all parallel lines in a picture lead to a single vanishing point creating the illusion of depth. This is called "perspective." Are you out of your depth trying to find Brunelleschi's hiding place?

In 1505, Pope Julius II commissioned Michelangelo to paint the ceiling of the Sistine Chapel in Rome. For almost five years, over an area 131 by 39 feet—roughly the size of a tennis court—Michelangelo lay on his back to paint 12 biblical scenes. He certainly deserved a rest. Rest assured, you'll find him here.

One of Michelangelo's most famous works is the 13-foot-high statue of *David*. He worked 20 hours a day for three years to carve the statue from marble. It shows his great understanding of the human body. Hammer away—find his two chisels.

Michelangelo Buonarroti, or Michelangelo (1475–1564), was one of the world's greatest sculptors. The *Pietà,* meaning "pity" in Italian, is his famous sculpture of Mary holding the lifeless body of her son Jesus. Inspired by Michelangelo, the famous painter, El Greco (1541–1614), painted his interpretation of this magnificent sculpture. It would be a pity not to find the painting of the *Pietà.*

By 1500, the Italian Renaissance had spread from Florence to Rome, where Raffaello Sanzio, or Raphael (1483–1520), was hired to paint four frescoes in the Vatican, headquarters of the Roman Catholic Church. Search the walls for his fresco called *School of Athens.*

The Renaissance reached its peak in the early sixteenth century. This period, known as the High Renaissance, lasted from about 1500 to 1527 and produced three masters—Leonardo da Vinci, Raphael, and Michelangelo. In this scene, where is da Vinci?

Leonardo da Vinci (1452–1519) was a painter, sculptor, architect, engineer, mathematician, scientist, and philosopher. His best-known painting is the *Mona Lisa*. She is famous for her mysterious smile. You'll be smiling when you find *Mona Lisa.*

His Wives and His Children

Between 1485 and 1603, a captivating and powerful family named Tudor ruled England. Many fascinating monarchs reigned during that time. The most intriguing was Henry VIII, who married six women while he was king and established a new religion in England.

The Wars of the Roses (1455–1487) between the House of Lancaster (symbolized by a red rose) and the House of York (symbolized by a white rose) were fought for the English crown. Finally, Henry Tudor of the House of Lancaster seized the throne and ended the war. Don't stop to smell the roses—find Henry Tudor.

Henry Tudor became Henry VII and began the House of Tudor, which reigned over England for more than a century. The Tudor rose was red and white, incorporating the symbols of both warring Houses. It's a thorny search for the Tudor Rose.

Henry VIII, Henry VII's son, ruled from 1509 to 1547. His first wife, Catherine of Aragon, gave birth to a daughter, Mary, but not a son. So Henry asked the Catholic Church for an official annulment of the mar-riage. The Church refused, so Henry started the Church of England. Try to come across a gold cross, a sacred symbol of Christianity.

Still seeking a male heir, Henry took a second wife, Anne Boleyn, a Protestant. She gave birth to Elizabeth in 1533. She failed to produce a son, but it was her reported flirting that angered Henry, so he ordered her beheaded. Do you see Anne hiding from Henry?

Henry soon married his third wife, Jane Seymour, who was also a Protestant. She gave Henry a son, but she died during childbirth. At last Henry had an heir, who later became King Edward VI. Look for the crying baby. He's the royal heir!

 Mary's half-sister, Elizabeth I, became queen in 1558. Under Elizabeth's rule, England remained Protestant, but she tolerated other religious faiths. Most of her reign was peaceful during which England became a powerful nation. Are you drawn to the portrait of Elizabeth I?

 At first, Queen Mary was popular, even among Protestants. But then she tried to restore the Catholic Church in England. She ordered the execution of those people who refused to convert to Catholicism, and so became known as Bloody Mary. Don't lose your head trying to find Mary's crown.

An attempt was made to place Edward's Protestant cousin, Lady Jane Grey, on the throne instead of Edward's Catholic sister, Mary. But the young and beautiful Lady Jane Grey instead was led to a wooden scaffold, where she took off her gloves before being executed for treason. Head for Lady Jane Grey's gloves before they fall into the wrong hands.

After Henry died, his son, Edward VI, inherited the throne at just nine years old. But he died of tuberculosis at the age of 16. During his reign, the first prayer book written in English, the *Book of Common Prayer,* was published in 1548. Come on, this book is easy to find.

 Katherine Parr, Henry's sixth and last wife, was a good stepmother to Henry's three children. She was also a caring nurse to Henry, who was now old and weakened by leg ulcers. She brought much festivity to the palace and spoke intelligently with visiting ambassadors. Care to look for Katherine reading one of her books?

 Henry agreed to marry Anne of Cleves, a Protestant, for political gain. But Henry said her father sent him a mare, not a princess. He had their marriage annulled after six months. Don't horse around—look for a mare with a yellow rose.

 At first, Henry showered Catherine Howard, his fifth wife, with gifts, but Catherine was more attracted to men her own age. So after just 17 months of marriage, she was beheaded for being unfaithful. Are you in over your head, or can you find this gift?

SAMURAI, SWORDS, AND SHOGUNS

The stage is set! But this is not your average school play—this is Kabuki, a traditional form of popular theater in Japan. Kabuki often depict events from Japanese history. This particular play is about the time of samurai, swords, and shoguns. So take your seat, and enjoy the show!

For many centuries, the Japanese believed their emperors were descended from the gods. Today, most Japanese are devoted to two religions—Shinto, based on the worship of ancestors, and Buddhism, which follows the teachings of the Buddha. A gate marking the entrance to a Shinto shrine is called a *torii*. On your tour, don't forget to stop at a torii.

The nobility lost much of its power when wealthy families acquired large areas of land. It's not easy to keep order in a country with many powerful leaders. In time, landowners and the Japanese government employed samurai warriors to keep order. Pay attention to a landowner giving coins to a samurai.

You would not want to mess with a samurai! They were known for their bravery. They were trained in fencing, wrestling, archery, and acrobatics. Samurai often carried two curved swords. Take a stab at finding six samurai swords with golden guards on the hilts.

Rugged mountains cover most of Japan, creating another reason for the emperor to hire samurai—they could move swiftly over the rough mountains on horseback. Use your horse sense to find a samurai on horseback in this scene.

By 1100, the Minamoto clan established a military government. The emperor gave the title of shogun to Minamoto Yoritomo (1147–1199). According to Japanese tradition, the family name is listed first. You may have to fight to find Minamoto in his warrior suit.

In 1868, the Tokugawa era ended, and Emperor Meiji became leader of Japan, ruling until his death in 1912. At the end of the Tokugawa shogunate, European military strength forced Japan to open its borders to the West. The Meiji dynasty promoted the adoption of Western technology. Can you find this emperor?

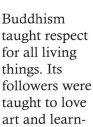

What's lurking in the shadows? It's a ninja! Feudal lords and samurai warriors hired these shadow assassins as spies from the 1300s to the 1600s. They could walk without making a sound, wore disguises to blend in with a crowd, and could scamper across trees and rooftops. Try to spy two ninjas.

Buddhism taught respect for all living things. Its followers were taught to love art and learning. They took pride in painting, writing, poetry, and flower arranging. Follow the fresh scent to the person arranging flowers.

Thousands of Japanese converted to Christianity. But in 1614, Tokugawa Ieyasu (1543–1616), who unified Japan and emerged as the shogun, outlawed Christianity because the Catholic priests had become involved in Japanese politics. Buddhism remained the country's official religion. Have faith in your search for two statues of the Buddha.

Powerful landholders were called *daimyo* (meaning "great name"). They controlled armies of samurai and large areas of land. Some daimyo even became more powerful than the emperor himself. Their armies used the new Portuguese weapons in battle. Take a shot at finding a samurai with a musket.

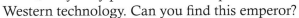

Minamoto's government was called a *shogunate,* which shared power with the emperor. Over the next 200 years, there would be many battles for power and no central Japanese government. Don't get lost trying to locate an ancient map of Japan.

In the mid-1500s, traders and priests from Portugal arrived in Japan. The traders sold goods and guns to the Japanese. The priests hoped to convert the Japanese to Christianity. Set your sights on three Portuguese priests.

The Melting Pot of America

"New York City's greatness," said former mayor Rudolph Giuliani, "is tied directly to the millions of immigrants who have come to build a better life for themselves and their families….We celebrate diversity as the common thread that binds us together." People of all nationalities and religious backgrounds make up the melting pot that is New York City.

When the Great Potato Famine struck Ireland between 1845 and 1852, Irish immigrants came to America searching for a better life. Many lived in the Battery in Lower Manhattan. They worked hard to put food on their tables. It's not an easy task to find a basket of potatoes in this scene.

The first St. Patrick's Day parade in New York City was held in 1762. Today, thousands come to watch it. The city even paints a green line, the color of luck for the Irish, down the middle of Fifth Avenue to mark the parade route. May the luck of the Irish be with you as you forage for three four-leaf clovers.

From 1892, the Federal Immigration Bureau used Ellis Island to register European immigrants, many of whom were Jews escaping persecution. Hasidic Jews wear black hats and beards and have curls (*payos*) down the sides of their faces. Tip your own hat to the Hasidic Jew in the crowd.

If you stroll through the Jewish community on New York's Lower East Side, you'll see many historic and religious sites, including the Eldridge Street Synagogue. The symbol of Judaism is a six-pointed star known as the Star of David. Point out the Star of David.

John Philip Sousa's parents met in New York City. His father was from Spain, and his mother was from Germany. The famous composer wrote many of America's favorite marching songs. March in time toward the famous bandmaster in this scene.

In 1924, Macy's was the largest department store in the United States. Because many of its employees were immigrants who missed the holiday traditions of their homelands, they started the Macy's Thanksgiving Day Parade. It is a celebrated symbol of New York City's melting pot. Salute the American flag in three places.

In 1990, the Ellis Island Immigration Museum opened. Today, visitors can follow the immigrants' footsteps from the ferry slip into the main building. Imagine their feelings of hope as they saw the Statue of Liberty from their ships. Feel free to look for two models of the Statue of Liberty.

Every year in mid-May, members of St. George Ukrainian Church in New York hold a Ukrainian Festival. They wear colorful Ukrainian costumes, perform folk dances, and serve authentic Ukrainian food. At the Ukrainian Museum, there's a special exhibition of *pysanky*—traditional hand-painted eggs. You don't have to walk on eggshells to find a painted ostrich egg.

By 1900, approximately 8,000 people were processed daily on Ellis Island and around 600 were housed in dormitories. After their stay on Ellis Island, many immigrants from the Odessa region in the Ukraine settled in Lower Manhattan. Take a step toward finding the Ukrainian woman who is mending a shoe.

One of the most important Chinese traditions is the Lion Dance. Two very strong men skilled at martial arts perform the dance. The Chinese also celebrate the Lantern Festival, which showcases many beautiful lanterns. It's really a bear to find a Panda on a lantern.

Today, Italians celebrate the Feast of San Genarro for ten days in September along Mulberry Street in Little Italy. The street festivities include parades, entertainment, food stands, and a cannoli-eating contest. Cannoli is a delicious Italian pastry. Can you find a cannoli?

In 1882, the U.S. government passed the Chinese Exclusion Act, but thousands already lived in New York City. A recognizable Chinese symbol is the yin-yang, which represents the feminine and masculine elements of nature. It's easy to find two of these symbols—they're in black and white.

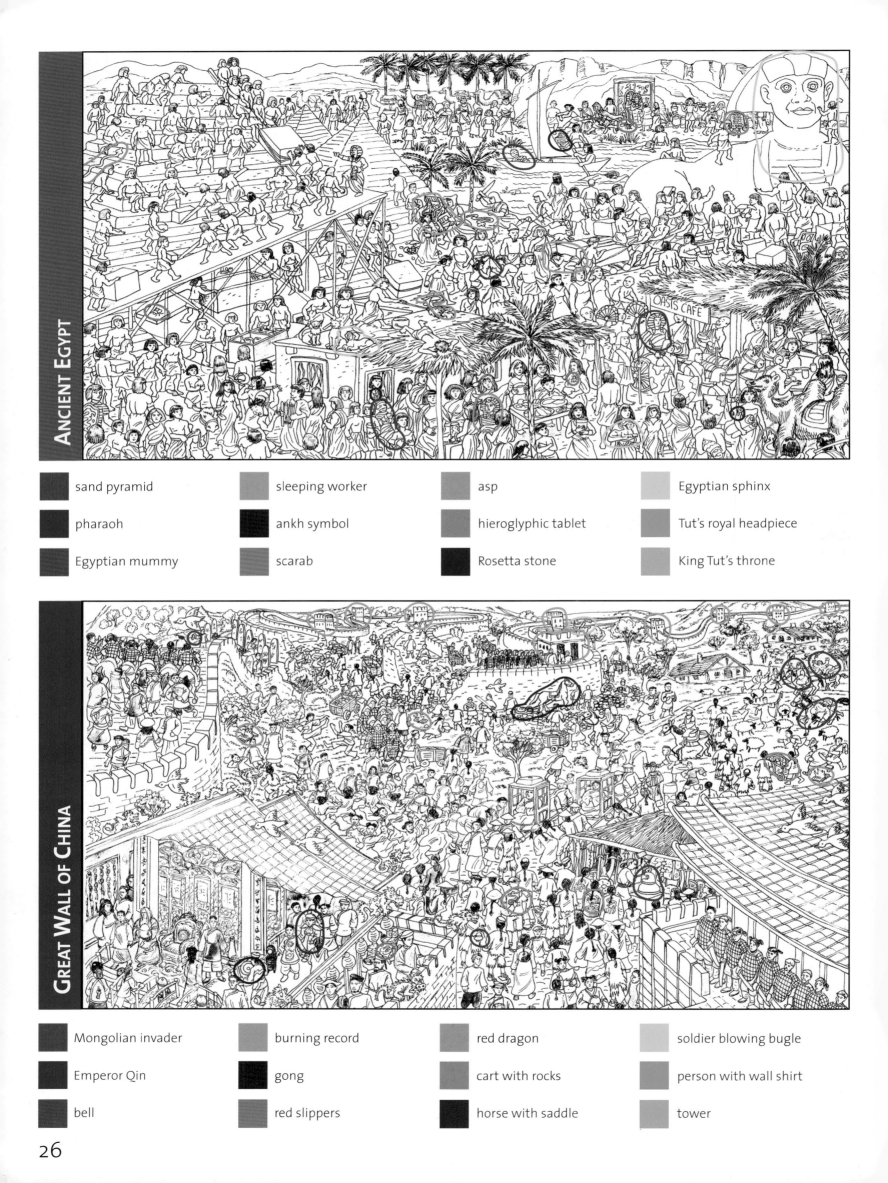

ANCIENT EGYPT

sand pyramid	sleeping worker	asp	Egyptian sphinx
pharaoh	ankh symbol	hieroglyphic tablet	Tut's royal headpiece
Egyptian mummy	scarab	Rosetta stone	King Tut's throne

GREAT WALL OF CHINA

Mongolian invader	burning record	red dragon	soldier blowing bugle
Emperor Qin	gong	cart with rocks	person with wall shirt
bell	red slippers	horse with saddle	tower

26

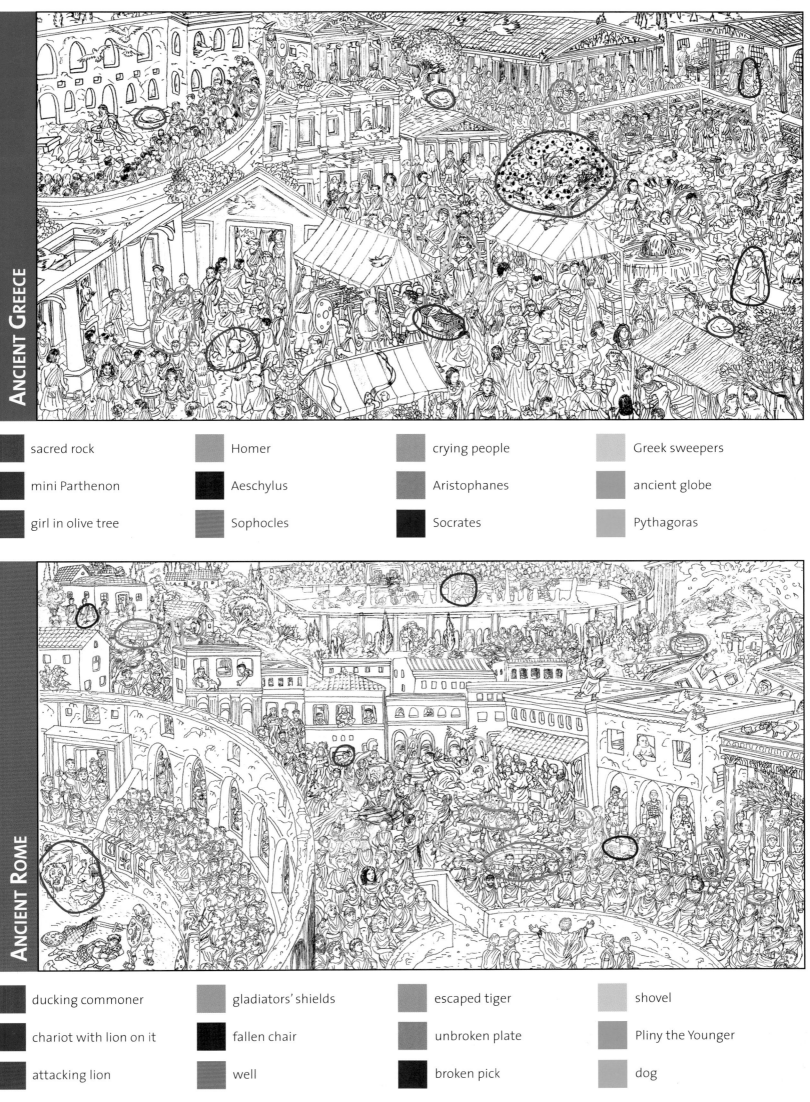

Ancient Greece

- sacred rock
- mini Parthenon
- girl in olive tree
- Homer
- Aeschylus
- Sophocles
- crying people
- Aristophanes
- Socrates
- Greek sweepers
- ancient globe
- Pythagoras

Ancient Rome

- ducking commoner
- chariot with lion on it
- attacking lion
- gladiators' shields
- fallen chair
- well
- escaped tiger
- unbroken plate
- broken pick
- shovel
- Pliny the Younger
- dog

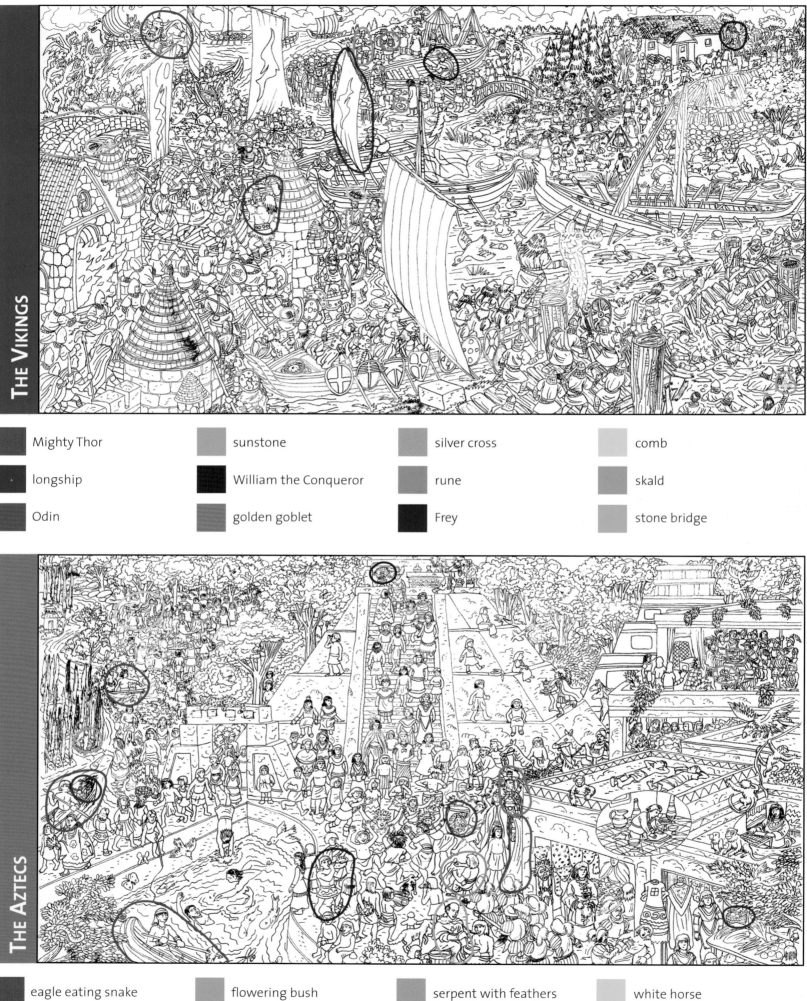

Mighty Thor		sunstone		silver cross		comb	
longship		William the Conqueror		rune		skald	
Odin		golden goblet		Frey		stone bridge	

eagle eating snake		flowering bush		serpent with feathers		white horse	
baskets of vegetables		Montezuma's crown		girl sewing a cloth		gold incense burner	
canoe		priest with stars on clothing		boy blowing into conch shell		Bartholome Casa	

Days and Knights

- archer
- black swan
- attacker
- beggar with a trencher
- Bible
- gauntlets
- lord of the castle
- lance
- eyeglasses
- chandler
- jester
- falcon

The Renaissance

- Apollo
- Duke of the Urbino portrait
- dog
- Filippo Brunelleschi
- Leonardo da Vinci
- Mona Lisa
- School of Athens fresco
- Pieta
- chisel
- Michelangelo

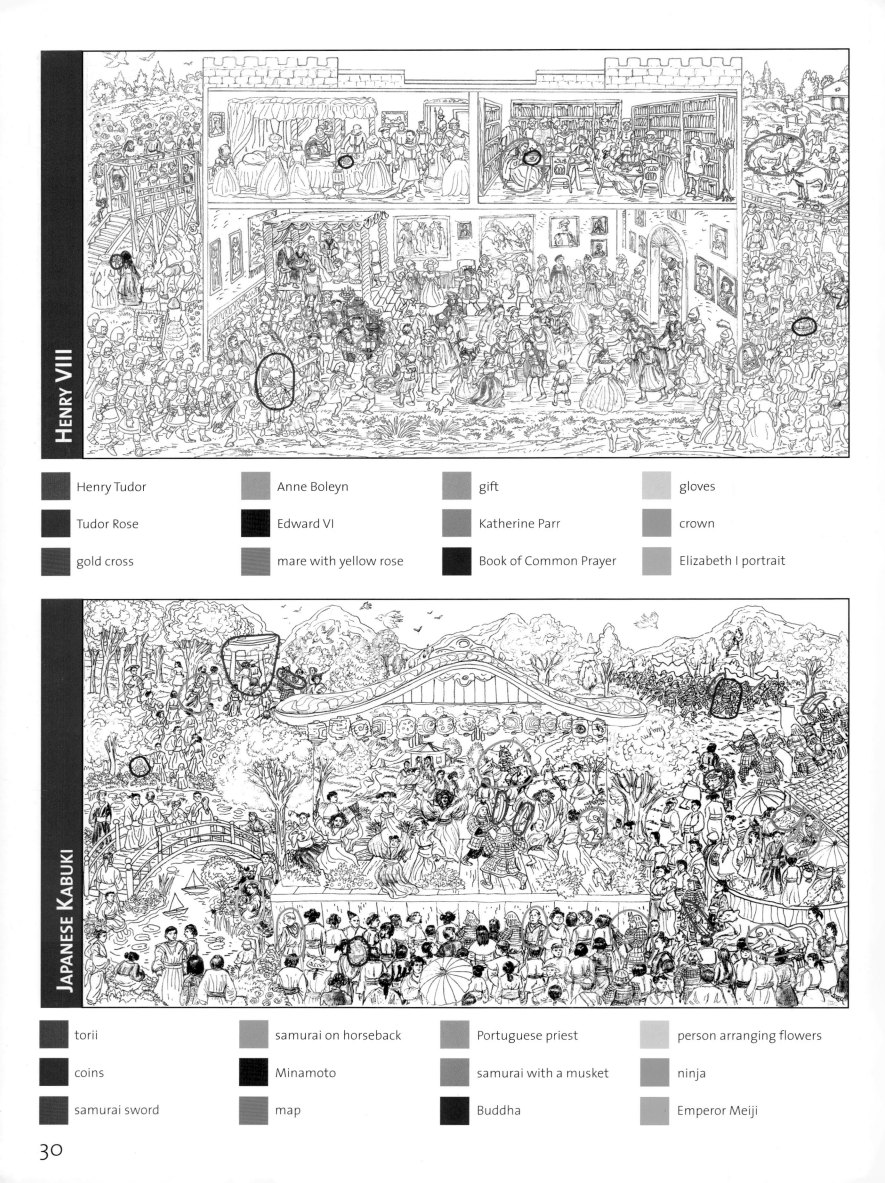

Henry Tudor

Anne Boleyn

gift

gloves

Tudor Rose

Edward VI

Katherine Parr

crown

gold cross

mare with yellow rose

Book of Common Prayer

Elizabeth I portrait

torii

samurai on horseback

Portuguese priest

person arranging flowers

coins

Minamoto

samurai with a musket

ninja

samurai sword

map

Buddha

Emperor Meiji

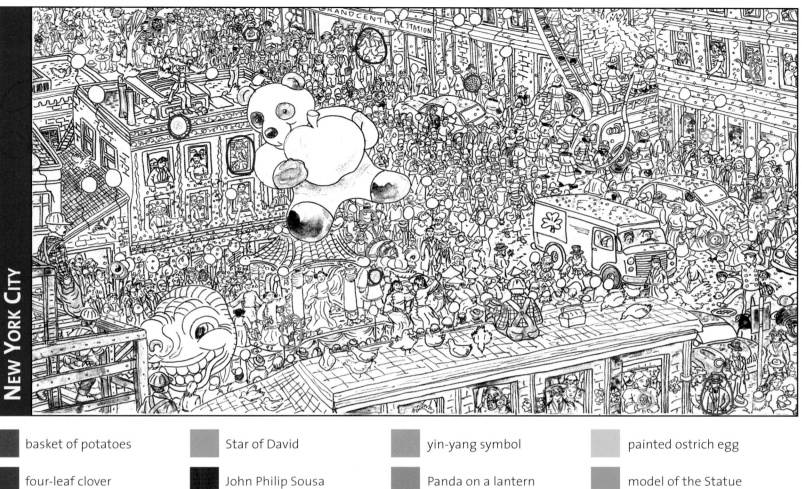

NEW YORK CITY

▪ basket of potatoes	▪ Star of David
▪ four-leaf clover	▪ John Philip Sousa
▪ Hasidic Jew	▪ cannoli

▪ yin-yang symbol	▪ painted ostrich egg
▪ Panda on a lantern	▪ model of the Statue of Liberty
▪ Ukrainian woman	▪ American flag

Look, Find & Learn Even More!

Think that's all there is? Not so fast! There's plenty more for you to find within these pages. Take the plunge—explore the scenes again to discover these cool items!

ANCIENT GREECE

The courts, temples, and theaters were located on the south slope of the Acropolis. There the Theater of Dionysus, the god of wine, presented the best plays of ancient Greece. Get to the theater on time by locating three sundials.

GREAT WALL OF CHINA

In 214 B.C., General Meng T'ien forced one million criminals, troublemakers, musicians, teachers, writers, artists, and peasants to march north to build the Great Wall. Are you drawn to the artist among the Chinese marchers?

THE VIKINGS

A longship had a rectangular sail and was outfitted with 32 oars. It could carry a crew of 15 to 20 men. The boats were so lightweight the Vikings could carry them on their shoulders when traveling over land. You won't have to travel far to find this Viking.

DAYS AND KNIGHTS

In Europe during the Middle Ages, when children reached age seven, they were sent to neighboring castles to be educated in music, dance, reading, and writing. They would also learn religion from a priest. Find the priest teaching the boys in the castle.

NEW YORK CITY

Ellis Island served as a barrier as well as a gateway. Immigrants too old or too weak to support themselves were often turned back. In 1924, a law was passed requiring immigrants to secure permits, called *visas*, from their homeland before coming to the United States. You don't need a pass to find the man holding a visa.

THE AZTECS

The town square was the center of Aztec activity in the daytime. It was filled with shops. Merchants sold gold and silver, feathers and fabric. Trappers sold jaguar, lion, and deer skins. There were tobacco sellers and food vendors selling turkeys, rabbits, and beans. Go to the jeweler, and look for this necklace in the Aztec scene.

THE RENAISSANCE

Leonardo da Vinci, a creative genius, was restless and often moved from one project to another, designing multibarreled guns, flying machines, a parachute, and a tank. He also brought a new element to oil painting. Instead of hard outlines on his figures, he blended shades of color. This smoky effect was called *sfumato*. Holy smoke, watch out for the parachute!

HENRY VIII

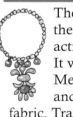

Under Henry VII, England became a stable nation. He ruled from 1485 to 1509. After Henry VII died, his son Henry became king. Henry VIII ruled from 1509 to 1547. His sister Margaret married the King of Scotland. Scotland is famous for bagpipes. Take a deep breath, and find three bagpipes.

ANCIENT EGYPT

The ancient Egyptians believed the Sphinx warded off evil spirits. Egyptian soldiers were on hand to keep out real intruders. Keep away from the soldier with a spear by the pyramid.